MANNERS
AT MEALTIME

JOSH PLATTNER

Consulting Editor, Diane Craig, M.A./Reading Specialist

Sandcastle

An Imprint of Abdo Publishing
abdopublishing.com

abdopublishing.com

Published by Abdo Publishing, a division of ABDO, PO Box 398166, Minneapolis, Minnesota 55439. Copyright © 2016 by Abdo Consulting Group, Inc. International copyrights reserved in all countries. No part of this book may be reproduced in any form without written permission from the publisher. SandCastle™ is a trademark and logo of Abdo Publishing.

Printed in the United States of America, North Mankato, Minnesota

062015
092015

Editor: Alex Kuskowski
Content Developer: Nancy Tuminelly
Cover and Interior Design and Production: Mighty Media, Inc.
Photo Credits: Shutterstock

Library of Congress Cataloging-in-Publication Data

Plattner, Josh, author.

Manners at mealtime / Josh Plattner ; consulting editor, Diane Craig, M.A./Reading Specialist.

pages cm. -- (Manners)

Audience: PreK to grade 3.

ISBN 978-1-62403-715-3

1. Table etiquette--Juvenile literature. 2. Etiquette for children and teenagers--Juvenile literature. I. Title.

BJ2041.P53 2016

395.5'4--dc23

2014046371

SandCastle™ Level: Transitional

SandCastle™ books are created by a team of professional educators, reading specialists, and content developers around five essential components—phonemic awareness, phonics, vocabulary, text comprehension, and fluency—to assist young readers as they develop reading skills and strategies and increase their general knowledge. All books are written, reviewed, and leveled for guided reading, early reading intervention, and Accelerated Reader™ programs for use in shared, guided, and independent reading and writing activities to support a balanced approach to literacy instruction. The SandCastle™ series has four levels that correspond to early literacy development. The levels are provided to help teachers and parents select appropriate books for young readers.

EMERGING · BEGINNING · **TRANSITIONAL** · FLUENT

CONTENTS

MANNERS AT MEALTIME

Good manners are great!
They are important.
Use them while you eat.

GETTING READY

Molly sets the table. She places spoons. She adds forks and knives. She puts the glasses on last.

EATING TOGETHER

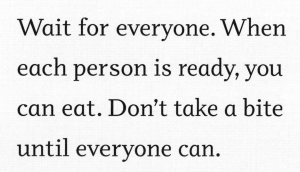

Wait for everyone. When each person is ready, you can eat. Don't take a bite until everyone can.

MOUTH MANNERS

Take small bites. Chew with your mouth closed. Keep your food in your mouth.

SUPER SEATING

Amy sits up straight. She keeps her chair legs on the floor. She keeps her **elbows** off the table.

PARTING POLITELY

It's okay to leave the table.
Ask before you leave. Say
"excuse me" when you get up.

CLEANING UP

Tammy clears the table. She takes the dishes. She puts them in the sink. She helps clean up!

RESTAURANT EATING

Be very **polite.** Always say "please" to your server. Say "thank you" too!

20

AT SCHOOL

Be friendly to others. Ask someone new to eat with you. Clear your place when you're done.

KEEP IT UP!

Always practice good manners at mealtime. Can you think of more? What else could you do?

GLOSSARY

elbow – a place on the arm where bones meet.

polite – having good manners or showing consideration for others.

restaurant – a place to buy and eat a meal.